IGBO METAPHYSICS

IGBO METAPHYSICS

The First Articulation
of African Philosophy of Being

by

Fr. Prof. E.M.P.
Edeh C.S.Sp.

AuthorHouse™ LLC
1663 Liberty Drive
Bloomington, IN 47403
www.authorhouse.com
Phone: 1-800-839-8640

First Edition: Madonna University Publications, 2009
ISBN 978-2166-92-8

Published by AuthorHouse   06/11/2014

ISBN: 978-1-4969-1898-7 (sc)
ISBN: 978-1-4969-1897-0 (e)

Library of Congress Control Number: 2014910595

Editing, Interior Design, and Digital Composition:
Josefina Ezpeleta

Cover Design:
Pedro Pablo Pérez Santiesteban

CONTENTS

INTRODUCTION

Some thirty years before the writing of the book *Towards an Igbo Metaphysics*, the basic question was: "Has Africa a philosophy"? From 1970 to 1976 my own thinking was this: We hear of European philosophy, American philosophy, Asian philosophy and Indian philosophy. I wonder, What of African philosophy? This motivated me to trace the history of African people and discover the following pertinent facts:

a. Africa, the second largest continent in the world, consists of a great block of ancient rock that has been little disturbed over two hundred million years, except for periodic uplifts and erosions. The topmost levels are the Mount Kenya (17,057 ft), the Kibo summit of Mount Kilimanjaro (19,341 ft), and the Mawenzi peak (16,889 ft).

b. From the most recent findings of archaeologists and palaeontologists, it is evident that Africa is historically the most senior of the seven continents of the world in the sense of sustaining human life. In fact, man's ancestors first become differentiated from primates in Africa.

c. By the Miocene times, a type of a creature known as *Kenyapithecus africanus* appeared in East Africa twenty million years ago having facial bone structure and dental arrangement like the modern man. This is indicative of the fact that a common ancestor for man and ape must have existed in Africa at least twenty million years ago.

d. The fossilized remains of *Homo habilis* and *Homo erectus,* who are the ancestors of man, were found in East Africa, near Victoria, about two million years ago.

e. From *Homo erectus* developed *Homo sapiens* (the modern man). By six to seven thousand years ago, the main racial types of human beings we have today were already settled down in Africa doing agriculture and stock raising.

Note that the archaeological findings do not contradict the biblical account of creation. The efforts of archaeologists and palaeontologists are nothing but human attempts at pinpointing where and when God breathed life giving breath (the soul) into man's nostril (*cf.* Gen. 2:7).

Of course it is difficult to locate the exact time and place of God's creation of man because God and His creative actions transcend time and place. He as the Creator alone knows the accurate chronology of all beings. Human beings can at best make intelligent guesses.

This brief discussion on the genesis of man in Africa helps us to understand how deep and original is African philosophy, which is typified in IGBO metaphysics. Hence, proper African philosophy cannot be said to be borrowed from Europe, America, Asia or India. With due respect to the biblical account of creation of man by God, man has lived in Africa from the earliest times. Thus it is right to say that African philosophy is as old as man.

The IGBOS

A brief historical account of the origin of the IGBOS—a distinguished part of the African people—shows that the IGBOS are of very ancient origin. Even at the end of the Stone Age, when Sahara dried up and became a desert, and people moved from Sahara to North and South of Africa, the IGBOS had settled in Nri-Awka and Isuama areas for a long period. Hence it is evident that IGBOS had developed independently from ancient times (*cf. Towards an Igbo Metaphysics,* pp. 10-14).

This knowledge of the ancient origin of the IGBOS helps us to understand the source of IGBO metaphysical thought-pattern. If the IGBOS came from another people, the originality of certain metaphysical principles will be attributed more or less to the IGBOS, depending on whether they were inherited from the very IGBOS or from the people from whom they migrated.

The ancient origin of the IGBOS helps us to comprehend the IGBO identity which designates the IGBOS as a people of their own with centuries of cultural development, an ancient race, a unique people with specific characteristics, a people with a copious supply of versatile common sense and a unique capacity for improvisation. They have a practical, unromantic approach to life and are characterized by a hardworking, enterprising and progressive nature (*cf. Towards an Igbo Metaphysics,* pp. 12-13).

Part One

CHAPTER ONE

Methodology

My aim in this work is not merely to discuss IGBO metaphysics as previous writers on African philosophy have been accustomed to do. Rather my aim is to actually engage in real IGBO metaphysics, to do it, that is, with an IGBO consciousness. Consequently the empirical method was used covering: (A) field work, and (B) specific method of articulation.

A. FIELD WORK

This was undertaken in two stages:

First stage.- Preliminary work (1974-1976), done among Nkanu people, a section of the IGBOS, a theological liturgical investigation into the people's respect for their ancestors and their traditional rites.

Second stage.- Research or investigation of IGBO metaphysics carried out in 1980. This was accomplished in three ways:

a. First way: Organizing over 300 appropriate questionnaires and interviewing various informants, e.g., Mazi Ede Oje, over 100 years old (*cf. Towards an Igbo Metaphysics,* p. 28), and Dr. Azuka A. Dike, on the biggest problem in IGBO meta-physics (*cf. Towards an Igbo Metaphysics,* p. 37).

b. Second way: Holding private discussions on my points of investigation with IGBO intellecttuals in universities in IGBO land and the rest of Nigeria, e.g., Prof. J. B. Schyler S.J. (Uni-versity of Lagos, HOD, Department of Sociology), who spent all his life studying Social Philosophy of Africans with particular reference to the Nigerian people.

c. Third way: From the discussions with Schyler, I moved to consult the Library of San Paolo di Apostolo in Rome, on works of IGBO scholars principally on religious and theological themes of IGBO culture, and Ann Arbor Microfilm Inter-national Center at the University of Michigan, USA, where I consulted various dissertations written by students from Nigeria and other African countries.

During these periods of investigations on African Philosophy in Nigeria, Africa, Europe and America I could not locate a case where anybody or scholar delved into the actual doing of African Philosophy through articulation of the metaphysics. All that writers on African philosophy were engaged in were discussions on the subject.

B. Method of Articulation

My field work and library research showed that no serious work had been done on Igbo metaphysics. Consequently, I had to undertake a work that is principally analytic and interpretative.

Analysis here is used in its root meaning of breaking through the thought-content of the language, culture and aspects of socio-religious practices of the Igbos in a quest for the metaphysical ground supporting them. As we analyze, we interpret, i.e. try to find some deeper meaning in the objects of our analysis.

This method includes:

- Linguistic analysis and interpretation;
- An analysis of the component parts of Igbo culture;
- Igbo religious practices. Religion is at the heart of Igbo man or woman.

Why this method of articulation?:

Because nothing had been written on this subject, I had to rely on analysis of the data gathered from my research questionnaires to gain some insight into Igbo thought. It is a pioneer work.

My instrument of investigation became:

a) Spoken Igbo, i.e. the names, idioms, proverbs, songs and stories;
b) Culture; and
c) Religious practices of the Igbo people.

The results of our research questionnaires provide us with the first hand information necessary to guarantee the originality and authenticity of this work on IGBO metaphysics.

Summarizing this chapter:

1. Our method of research is analytic and interpretative:
   a. This is required by the nature of the work, a pioneer work. Language, religious practices and culture are the data, which we must investigate.
   b. These are not the goals but the tools for our investigation.
   c. Our interest lies in the metaphysical thought, which we get into through an analysis of their language, religion and cultural practices.
   d. Our interpretation leads us to the metaphysical plane, the ultimate springboard, and the final source of action of the IGBOS' way of life.

2. Our interpretation is theoretically and practically oriented:

Theoretically:

Because as a philosophical investigation it is principally a quest for pure understanding.

Practically:

Because we survey the results of our investigation with a view to the interplay between thought and action. It behoves modern philosophical endeavour to aim at not only theoretical achievements but also at practical results.

CHAPTER TWO

A Description of Metaphysics

First of all, some necessary definitions:

PHYSICS refers to the study of nature in general and meta-physics comes after it.

METAPHYSICS is beyond physics (*cf.* Aristotle's classification of the Sciences). Metaphysical questions arise out of but go beyond, factual or scientific questions about the world.

Traditionally, metaphysics includes:

   a. Cosmology
   b. Ontology
   c. Theodicy

a. *Cosmology* discusses the origin, structure and space-time relations of the universe.
b. *Ontology* asks what is the "reality" of propositions and numbers. Is existence a predicate or a property?
c. *Theodicy* relates to the philosophy of religion and deals with questions such as: Does anything exist necessarily? Why is there something rather than nothing?

Fr. Prof. E.M.P. Edeh C.S.Sp.

A DISTINCTIVE FEATURE OF METAPHYSICS

Is the universality of its questions the distinctive feature of metaphysics?

It seeks an inventory of the kinds of things that exist, but most importantly, asks what can be said about anything that exists in so far as it exists.

Questions involving the relations between very general notions such as: thing, entity, object, individual, universal, particular substance, event, process, state, etc., all constitute a special field of metaphysical investigation.

Genesis of Metaphysics

Here we distinguish four major outlooks:

- a) Platonic Outlook
- b) Aristotelian Outlook
- c) Heraclitian Outlook
- d) Edeh Outlook (*Ife-di, cf. Towards an Igbo Metaphysics*)

Platonic Outlook

It is connected with attitude towards change.

It takes change on the basis of the universe.

The fact of change led Plato to investigate enduring reality and our knowledge of it.

In his group are: Parmenides, Spinoza and the Monists.

They maintained that either change is not fully real or that the most basic things do not really change.

Aristotelian Outlook

It was formulated to understand change.

Aristotle postulated potency and act as the substantive basis of all that is.

From Aristotle are derived the important distinctions:

- Essence and Existence
- Matter and Form
- Substance and Accidents

Heraclitian Outlook

It takes events and processes as the basis of the universe. In the group of Heraclitus are: the Stoics, Hegel, Bergson, Whitehead and Nietzsche.

For them, change is at the heart of all things.

For Nietzsche: "change is an eternal recurrence of the same cycle, and endless repetition of exactly the same world history." Unity and constancy are accepted as real in so far as they depend essentially on change.

Edeh Outlook

Ife-di was formulated as the most appropriate rendering of the concept of being. It covers all categories of entities, visible and invisible and covers the note of existence commonly associated with being.

Note that:

a. The examination of the nature and kinds of change reveals the impact of the distinctions between potency, act, privation, matter and form.

b. These distinctions lead us to the question of matter and substance and their relations to space and time.

c. The distinctions of space and time open up a whole dimension of problems regarding the reality, nature, absoluteness, and uniqueness of space and time.

d. The discussion of space and time in metaphysics inevitably involves one in the question of infinity: Is the universe finite or infinite? Did it have a beginning in time or was it eternal?

Through the centuries these questions have agitated the minds of religious thinkers.

The history of Western metaphysics echoes the debates on these topics handled at various levels by Neoplatonists, early and medieval Christians, Muslims and Jews.

Summarizing this chapter:

From this brief sketch of the areas covered by Western metaphysics, one thing is clear: namely, that metaphysics is a search for an understanding of beings in their ultimate causes.

It seeks a description and identification of the intelligible nature, structure and characteristic qualities of reality. As a search for meaning, metaphysics is an inquiry into the intelligibility and value of reality. Bearing in mind this description of metaphysics together with the areas it covers, let us now approach IGBO metaphysics with an IGBO mind, "freed as far as possible from the presuppositions and controversies of Western philosophical thought."

My Use of Igbo Language and Culture

There are two main avenues to the thought-content of any people, namely, its language and culture.

The philosophy of a people can be stated as the underlying principles of the people's way of life as expressed in language and culture. Realizing their importance I treated the language and culture of the IGBOS as a way into IGBO Metaphysics. In fact it is through language and culture that IGBO Metaphysics or any African philosophy is preserved and transmitted.

Consequently I endeavoured to extract elements of metaphysics from IGBO language and culture, and particularly from certain religious practices.

CHAPTER THREE

The Origin, Structure and Purpose of the Universe

THE ORIGIN OF THE UNIVERSE

An IGBO proverb says: *Ife welu mbido g' enwe njedebe,* which means "Whatever has a beginning will have an end."

From the observance of the process of the coming-to-be and ceasing-to-be of visible reality, one draws the obvious inference: Whatever has a beginning has an end.

Therefore the visible world has a beginning. Hence the IGBO mind reasons to the possibility of a beginning for all visible entities.

N` oge gboo gboo is a familiar expression used to refer to the very distant time when there was nothing in existence, a time prior to the beginning of beginnings.

The origins are always traced back to the land of the unseen and visible objects are to be understood as gifts from the head of the inhabitants of the unseen.

Note: A sample IGBO account of the origin of visible things is the account of the Origin of Fire. (*cf. Towards an Igbo Metaphysics,* p. 72).

This shows that even though the IGBOS see material realities coming to be and ceasing to be, they know that there is an unseen which serves as the basis of the movement of coming-to-be and ceasing-to-be.

Thus we see the relationship between the unseen beings and the fact of the origin of the visible realities: The visible realities have their origin in the unseen beings, the inhabitants of the invisible world. Thus the IGBOS believe in:

a) The *existence* of two worlds:

Uwaa

Uwa N'ani muo

Uwaa n' uwa ozo.

This is typified in the invocations of *igo ofo* (morning prayer) with a cup of palm wine by the traditional IGBO man or elder with his family in the morning.

b) The idea of *reincarnation*: "Reincarnation to most Africans, is a good thing. It is a return to this sunlit world for a further period of invigorating life," says E.G. Parrinder (*cf. Towards an Igbo Metaphysics*, p. 74)

c) The IGBO concept of *death*: For the IGBOS, death is not an end but a transition. If a person dies, he/she is born into another life completely diferent from the one he/she had. This is the case with the ancestors. There must be a world other than this visible world where the ancestors are dwelling from, where they exercise some influence on the goings and comings of the living. Hence there must be two worlds.

d) The *theory of duality*: IGBO idea of the existence of two worlds leads to IGBO theory of duality, which says: "For all beings in the material universe, existence is a dual and interrelated phenomenon." Whatever exists in a sensible form in this world has a dual existence, that is, the reality of its existence is a phenomenon in the visible world and also a reality in the invisible world. Whatever obtains here has its replica in the world of the unseen.

THEORY OF DUALITY AND THE SOUL-BODY UNITY IN MAN

The IGBO idea of the existence of two worlds has its deeper understanding in the theory of duality, which leads to the IGBO way of grappling with the old philosophical problem of the soul-body unity in man. (*cf. Towards an Igbo Metaphysics,* p. 83).

The IGBO theory of duality maintained in a sharp sense leads to an impasse with regard to the question of the soul-body unity in man. But when the same theory is considered in an inverted sense, it seems to handle the problem.

IGBO Theory of What Makes a Thing-to-be (*Ife melu ife ji di*)

Cf. Towards an Igbo Metaphysics, page 84.

From my encounter with my informant, Mazi Ede Oje, who was over 100 years old (*cf. Towards an Igbo Metaphysics,* p. 84), an *nze*, who is an embodiment of traditional wisdom, a link between the past and the present, it is clear that in IGBO thought there are four things that are involved in the process of the coming-to-be of any sensible object. Viz:

1. *Ife ana afu anya na emetu aka*

    The visible and tangible

2. *Nke zolu ezo*

    The hidden (invisible)

3. *Onye nka*

    The artisan

4. *Ife kpatalu*

    The purpose

These are the four principal elements in an IGBO theory of what makes a thing to be. The first and second need no further explanation since they flow from the IGBO theory of duality.

The third is not identical with the object in the process of coming-to-be example of the fire and the sender, in the case of the illustration of the origin of fire. Note that *Onye nka* (artisan) can be seen in two ways: either visible or invisible.

The IGBOS have the basic conception that the process of the coming-to-be of any object, be it material or immaterial, is *mediately* and *ultimately* the work of the inhabitants of the unseen world.

Mediately:

Because in the act of the coming-to-be of any object, the head of the inhabitants of the unseen world mediates between the artisan and the object under production.

Ultimately:

Because it is through the creative power of the head of the inhabitants of the unseen world that all ability comes, even the ability of the artisan to produce an object. Hence the IGBOS say that the process of the coming-to-be of any object has its ultimate source in Him (the head of the inhabitants of the unseen world).

The fourth element, the purpose of matter (*ife Kpatalu*) is seen as the sum total of the four elements. In the daily parlance of IGBO, the expression *ife Kpatalu* can refer to the totality that makes an object in question to be. It also refers to the specific purpose of the object.

For the IGBOS the purpose of a thing determines its being. Whatever has no immediate purpose is regarded as worthless. Its being is questionable. From the purpose (*uru obalu*) one reasons back to the validity of its being. If a thing is of any use, then it is worth being.

From the theory of *Ife melu ife ji di* (what makes a thing to be), we know that IGBO thought recognizes the universal question involved, namely: how a material object moves from the state of non-being to the state of being.

CRITICAL REFLECTIONS

Some merits and demerits of IGBO thinking:

1. The IGBO theory of duality as applied to the problem of the universals treats it in at least embryonic form.

2. In the question of the soul-body unity in man the theory, taken sharply (i.e. sharp duality) leads to an impasse. But the inverted version of the theory of duality provides a possible solution.

3. One of the greatest merits of IGBO thought at this point is its attempt to explain the origin of material things: Everything in the material world is created by the head of the inhabitants of the unseen world.

All that we have in the forgoing pages have paved our way to the proper understanding of IGBO metaphysics as the first articulation of African philosophy.

Part Two

CHAPTER FOUR

An Igbo Understanding of Being

CONCEPT OF BEING IN THE IGBO LANGUAGE

There are 2 hypotheses: Onye hypothesis and Ife hypothesis.

Onye Hypothesis: Onye conveys the idea of a human being and can be employed to designate spiritual beings. But the concept cannot include inanimate, vegetable, or non-inanimate entities. Hence Onye is not comprehensive enough to translate the term being.

E.g.	*Onye ozo*	another
	Onye Okike	creator
	Onye nzuzu	a fool

Ife Hypothesis: "*Ife*" primarily means "thing", material or immaterial.

E.g.	*Ife obuna*	anything, whatever
	Ife ojoo	evil thing
	Ife ma ife	the wise

According to Ife hypothesis there is no other word in IGBO language that approximates IGBO concept of being: I accept this for the following metaphysical reasons:

a. The IGBO notion of "being" is all embracing covering all categories of being.

b. Primarily, it refers to inanimate entities like English "thing".

c. But by an expansion of meaning it is used to designate human, supra human, inanimate, vegetable and non-human animate entities.

Kedu Ife kelu ife	Who created things?

("*Ife*" can be affixed to any adjective or verb to mean specific thing.)

Kedu ife melu njo n'uwa?	Ego
Kedu ife melu ego?	Man

It is very important to note that:

(a) It is clear that the IGBOS readily use the concept "*Ife*", in

- a particular sense to mean "thing" referring to inanimate being; and

- an universal sense to mean any being at all: material or immaterial, inanimate or animate, human or non-human.

(b) *"Ife"* does not bring out the important aspect of being, i.e. the fact of existence. It does not cover both existent and non-existent entities.

(c) Solution: *"Ife"* can be affixed to any adjective or to a verb to mean a specific thing. The IGBO verb "to be" is *"idi"*, and, used as an adjective can be suffixed to anything to show that it exists, for example:

Okwute-di	The Stone that is
Osisi-di	The tree that is
Chukwu-di	God who is

"Idi" used with *"Ife"* means anything at all that is in existence.

Hence *Ife-di* is the most appropriate IGBO rendering of the concept of being. Why?

Ife-di covers all categories of entities namely: visible and invisible etc., and covers the note of existence which is commonly associated with being.

Categories of *Ife-di* and Their Subcategories

Categories	Subcategories	
Supra sensory	*Chineke*	
	Ndi muo	The unseens
Human	*Ndi din du*	The living
	Ndi nwuru	The dead
Thing	*Anu*	Animals as distinguished from human and inanimate beings

Thing (cont.)	*Ife nkiti nwelu ndu*	All animals entities
	Ife nkiti enweghi ndu	All inanimate entities
	Ogu	Beings that have no existence of their own. Their being depends on a collection of interaction of different things placed together.

E.g.: What a *Dibia* makes is *Ogu*.

Being and man's understanding of being

The IGBO idea of what is follows the two fold division of the universe: the visible and the invisible.

Confronted with the question: How do you become aware of what is?, the IGBO would say that an awareness of what is begins with an awareness of man as a visible concrete instance of what exists.

QUESTIONNAIRE TO MAZI EDE OJE

Q- *Gini bu Ife-di?* (What is being?)

A- *Ife-di bu Ife-di.* (Being is being.)

Q- *Gini di?* (What is?)

A- *Ife nine bu Ife-di.* (All things are beings.)

Q- *Kedu k'isi malu na Ife-di?* (How do you know that beings are?)

Fr. Prof. E.M.P. Edeh C.S.Sp.

A- *Emegi ife ozo, amalum nkea maka na madu di, maka n' anyi di.* (I know this at least from the fact that human beings are, we are.)

Q- *Kedu uzo isi ama ife bu n' ife di?* (How do you know what it is that beings are?)

A- *Ofu uzo bu site na ima ife bu na madu di.* (One way is by knowing what it is that man is.

First Answer of My Informant

Note that the first answer—Being is being—is a tautology yet it brings out an important point. A tautology of this type is used by IGBO Elder to indicate that what he is talking about cannot be defined.

In saying that "being is being" my informant is acknowledging the fact that even though "being" is a common concept, cannot be defined in the way ordinary concepts are defined.

St. Thomas Aquinas in his *De Veritate* also observed this when he said that "being" cannot be defined in the way essences are defined. We cannot, strictly speaking form an essential idea of "being". It is the most evident concept to which every other concept is reducible.

From the first answer of my informant, one can understand the IGBO mind struggling with the perennial problem of how to grasp what it is "to be". Not knowing what to do, he states it in a tautological form.

Heidegger warned against this, that is, over simplifying "being" into an empty concept.

My references to Aquinas and Heidegger show that the IGBOS bear witness to the philosophical tradition of maintaining that "being" is not an essence and hence cannot be defined as an essence is defined, by genus and specific difference.

Second Answer of My Informant

Here he takes a step further—All things are beings. This is a way of stating that the notion of "being" penetrates all other contents. Hence it is present in the formulation of every concept. This is in keeping with the view of Bernard Lonergan who said that the notion of "being" is unique, for it is the core of all acts of meaning (*cf. Towards an Igbo Metaphysics*, p. 99).

Note that the views of Heidegger and Lonergan corroborate the IGBO uncertainty at this point regarding a defined notion of "being". In the Western tradition dating from Aristotle, "being" is not an essence and therefore it is indefinable.

Third Answer of My Informant

Here my informant answering the question: How do you know that beings are?, takes a dramatic turn, saying "I know this at least from the fact that human beings are, we are,"

In this, the IGBO is suggesting that a notion of "being" could derive from our concept of "man". If so the questions are:

> (1) What is there in the concept of "man" that will respect both the diversity and unity of "being"?

(2) What is common in all being is the act of existence. But how do we move to this common notion from a concept of "man"?

Now let us look closely at the IGBO word for "man" (the human): *madu.*

Etymologically *"madu"* is a short form of *mmadi* (*mma-di*), where *mma* is the IGBO word for good, a good, or the good, and *di* is from *idi,* which is the IGBO verb "to be."

E.g: *Okwute-di*   The stone that exists (is).

         Osisi-di   The tree that exists (is).

Hence a combination of *mma* and *di* is *mma-di,* which means "good that is."

From this exposition of the meaning of the word for man—*madu*—we discover that in man the IGBO is able to discern the notion of "good that is."

At this point two questions must be answered:

(1) How are we to understand "good that is"?

(2) How far does this notion respect the diversity of "being"?

Let's answer the question number 1: The IGBO notion of "good that is" must be understood in the context of creation: for the IGBO the notion of "good" is derived from divine creation. To say that man is the "good that is", is not to say that man is "good in se", for no one is good in se except God. This is brought out in IGBO expressions like: *so Chukwu di mma ezie* (only God is good in the true sense).

For the IGBOS man's goodness is participated. Man is "good that is" in the sense that, having been created by God, he is a product of his maker. Hence, man shares in the being of his maker, the highest good.

From the expressions like *Iketa n'ife* and *Isolu n'ife* we know that in the IGBO mentality whereas man shares in the being of God as "good that is," man is not "good in se".

And now, the answer for the question number 2: How the notion of "good that is" respects the diversity of being is clearly seen when the notion is predicated of not only man, but also other particular things. For example:

> This stone is good that is
>
> This tree is good that is
>
> Something is good that is

The generalized statement here does not leave out the particularity of the individual objects. The existence of a "being" is what makes it a "being".

So the judgement, "something is good that is," respects that which makes each object a being and yet it can be applied to any object.

This application is possible on the basis that all things are created by God and hence, the notion of "good that is" can be attributed to them.

Two important issues that arise here are:

(1)   Is IGBO metaphysics a pantheism?

(2)   The problem of Evil.

Fr. Prof. E.M.P. Edeh C.S.Sp.

Here we restrict ourselves to the second issue leaving the first to be discussed somewhere else in another work.

THE PROBLEM OF EVIL

Even though the IGBOS regard being as the "good that is" they are not so naïve as to believe that there are no evils in the world. The fact that all beings are good in the ontological sense makes the question of moral evil crucial. What of the perennial problem of moral and physical evil? The IGBO ontological position that all things are good because of creation presupposes two things:

- First, that God is the absolute good who causes the good in all beings.
- Second, that God's very act of creating is synonymous with his act of causing good in what he creates.

In other words, by the very fact of its being created, a creature is good in a participated sense. Hence the question is how is it that there is evil in the world? Evils that sometimes cover man's consciousness with darkness and despair?

All said and done, for the IGBOS, a possible way of reconciling the presence of evil in the world with God's goodness and causality is to realize:

(a) That God does not cause evil proximately; and

(b) Even in the remote sense He does not cause evil since He originally created the proximate causes of evil not as evil but as good.

Summarizing this chapter regarding the IGBO understanding of "being":

We began with a search for a concept of "being" in the IGBO language. We came up with *Ife-di* as the most appropriate concept covering all visible and non-visible entities and including existence, which is common to all beings.

An idea of the IGBO awareness of what is, begins with an understanding of man as an instance of what exists. Hence we went to analyze the IGBO concept of man as "good that is". Applying this to individual instances of beings, we were able to arrive at a generalized statement that enables us to make the judgement: "Being is something that is", or "good that is." This is the general way of expressing the being of each individual as well as the common intelligibility of all beings.

IGBO awareness of "being" is not restricted to man but covers all beings, because the IGBO idea of goodness is not limited to man. Why? The source of goodness is God, the supreme goodness.

The basis of any creature's being good is the fact of creation. Therefore all creatures in so far as they are created beings participate in goodness. Hence IGBO awareness of "being" covers all beings.

At this juncture a pertinent question is:

What we have in *Towards an Igbo metaphysics*, is it a metaphysics, an IGBO metaphysics? In other words, with this study, is there any such thing as an IGBO metaphysics as there is, for instance, Greek or German metaphysics? If it is a metaphysics, is it truly an African metaphysics?

I hereby state categorically that there is such a thing as an IGBO metaphysics. What we have done in this work is nothing but a pioneer's work of a formal articulation of IGBO metaphysics.

It is not a metaphysics as done by an IGBO. What is metaphysics if not one's God-man-world conceptual scheme or relationship, how one understands and interprets this scheme, what this scheme means to one and how one's being, life and existence are determined by the relationship involved.

We have seen an articulated form of IGBO concept of this God-man-world relationship. The IGBOS understand and interpret this relationship in a way specific to them. For example the IGBO mentality did not require any outside indoctrination to arrive at the fact that everything in the material universe has a being in the world of the unseen. The IGBOS show this in the mystical story of the origin of fire.

In the IGBO understanding and interpretation of life and existence, beings and being, the IGBO mentality opens the question of being from the IGBO notion of man as *mma-di*, that is "good that is". This gives the IGBO mind the clue to a general notion of "being" as "good that is" because of having been created by *Chi-ne-ke*.

A closer study of *Chi-ne-ke* reveals that he is the ultimate source of being, life and existence, and yet he is *Chi-ukwu*, the almighty. So the IGBO mentality has its unique way of understanding the God-man-world scheme: All things including man are "goods that are" because they are created by God who is *Chi-ne-ke*, *Ose-bu-luwa* and *Chi-ukwu*.

In this respect there must be such a thing as IGBO metaphysics and since it is this IGBO way of understanding the God-man-world relationship that is articulated here, it is correct to say that what we have in this work is IGBO metaphysics. It is IGBO manner of questioning with respect to the meaning of reality, being, life and existence. In the face of the mysteries of life that surround him, the IGBO begins to wonder: What does it mean to be? A clue to the answer comes from the IGBO notion of man as *mma-di* (good that is). To be is to be the "good that is"? Why would beings be the "goods that are"? Here the IGBO questioning mind arrives at the fact that beings are the "goods that are" because they are created by God who is *Chi-ne-ke*, *Ose-bu-luwa* and *Chi-ukwu*.

The meaning of reality is thus discovered in an IGBO way: God is the meaning of reality, for He is the ultimate source and end of being. Man is created to be free and yet dependent on his creator.

The whole universe has a purpose for its creation and is guided by God to the fulfillment of this purpose. All this is the manner of IGBO questioning which is strictly metaphysical. This is what we have seen articulated in this work, *Igbo metaphysics*.

Part Three

CHAPTER FIVE

African Philosophy Typified in Igbo Metaphysics

In IGBO METAPHYSICS, the first articulation of African philosophy, I have presented a true metaphysics, namely: the African man's God-man-world conceptual scheme or relationship, how the African understands and interprets this scheme, what this scheme means to him and how his being, life and existence are determined by the relationship involved.

For the Africans, as typified in IGBO METAPHYSICS, there is a relationship between the unseen beings and the fact of the origin of the visible realities: The visible realities have their origin in the unseen beings, the inhabitants of the invisible world. Thus the Africans hold on to the existence of two worlds, *uwaa n'uwa ozo*.

This is manifested in the invocations of *igo ofo* (morning prayer) with a cup of palm wine by the traditional IGBO man with his family in the morning.

From the African understanding and interpretation of life and existence, beings and Being, the question of being is opened up from the African notion of man as *mma-di*, "the good that is." From there, the African arrives at a general notion of being as "good that is" because of having been created by *Chineke* (God the Creator), who is the ultimate source of being, life and existence, the *Chi-ukwu*, the Almighty.

The distinctive feature of African metaphysics (as it is clear in IGBO METAPHYSICS) is that its notion of being is drawn from the concept of man and, at the same time, it is a theological metaphysics. In deriving the African notion of being from a concept of man, African metaphysics has also presented itself as a religious metaphysics giving a witness to man as *Homo religiosus*.

African philosophy as indicated in the book *Peace to the Modern World* (2007), is characterized by the fact that in it one is dealing with a practical theoretical science in the sense that by nature, African metaphysics is a lived philosophy rather than a purely theoretical or scientific venture. From a deep consideration of the African culture, language, socio-religious milieu and above all, a holistic view of the universe, this metaphysics leads us to behold man as dignified.

THE IDEAL OF HUMAN DIGNITY

For one to capture and present what is truly an African way of viewing life and existence, beings and Being, one has to come to grips with the interplay of thought and action. For the African, philosophy is the way of life expressed in the peoples' rituals, language, and other cultural manifestations. This philosophy gives people the ideal of human existence, and specifically an ideal of human dignity based upon the belief that all beings created by God are ontologically good and deserve respect. Man, who is a *Homo religious,* is cared for and supported by God. Hence he enjoys a position of high dignity conferred on him from creation.

In African metaphysics, the attentive mind discerns a reflection of that God-man-world scheme. It is this God-man-world scheme that is clearly presented in IGBO METAPHYSICS. And it is this that gives credence to the dignity of human beings and human existence. African metaphysics is saying that we should accept man as good within the context of creation.

AFRICAN THEORY OF DUALITY

This ideal of human dignity is manifested in African theory of duality, which maintains that: For all beings in the material universe, existence is a dual and inter-related phenomenon. Whatever exists in a sensible form in this world has a dual existence, that is, the reality of its existence is a phenomenon in the visible world, and also a reality in the invisible world. Whatever obtains here has its replica in the world of the unseen.

a. The theory of duality is exemplified in the African ways of choosing a marriage partner: The principle underlying the African method of making this choice is based on the notion of life and existence. In making a decision to marry, the young man knows that he is taking a normally irrevocable step to bring a new life into his community of being.

b. Within this community of being are the two main divisions in the African concept of the universe, viz: *Uwa* (the world of the visible) and *Ani muo* (the world of the unseen), that is *uwa n' uwa ozo*.

Hence life, the existence that is added through marriage to the family of a man, becomes a phenomenon, an event taking place in the visible world because it involves visible and sensible entities. But it does not end there. Whatever happens here occurs likewise in the sphere of the unseen.

The two-fold community of being of the woman is handed over to a new community of being in both the visible and invisible realm. Since this transfer of life and existence is affected on two levels, the wills of both —the visible and the invisible—are meticulously sought before marriage is contracted and once marriage is contracted it is regarded as sacred and hence, indissoluble.

THE AFRICAN CONCEPTS OF ULTIMATE BEING

Africans conceive the "ultimate being" as:

1. *Chi-ne-ke,* one who creates and is actually present in his creatures.

2. *Ose-bu-luwa,* one who has a plan for each creature and an objective plan for the entire creation, and who at the same time, guides and directs the creatures to the realization of the purpose of their creation. Thus, the active presence of God in the beings of experience means His care and support of these beings to the realization of their purpose.

3. The "ultimate being" is not only *Chi-ne-ke* and *Ose-bu-luwa.* He is also *Chi-ukwu,* that is, the highest in an absolute sense, the unlimited fullness of being, the Supreme Being, the fullness of life, whose perfection is boundless (*cf. Towards an Igbo Metaphysics,* pp. 132-133). This brings us to the question of theology in the African context, but will be treated in detail not here but in another work.

Suffice it to say that since being is conceived as "good that is" and the African metaphysics accepts the being of beings, that is, the ultimate source of being as *Chi-ne-ke* (one who creates), then African mind proceeds naturally from metaphysics to theology as the study of God and his dealings with beings. African mind aims at a general notion of being as "good that is". The being is, because it has been created by *Chi-ne-ke,* the ultimate source of being, life and existence.

In the realm of theology, the African mind conceives being as "good that is" because man is said to be good in so far as he is being created by the Ultimate Being (*Chi-ne-ke*), who is also *Ose-bu-luwa.* Within this context, man is seen in the concept of God creating him and at the same time being cared for by God. This confirms the mystery of man's dealing with God.

From my articulation of African metaphysics, I mean that this affirmation of man as "good that is" based on the fact that he is created and cared for by God, must be concretized in practical terms. Thus, the caring as part of the mystery of man's dealing with God must permeate truly from God-man relationship to man-man relationship.

Hence, the principle in African religious mind, whereby man is his brother's keeper, leads to the ideal of human dignity in the interplay between thought and action, which characterizes African philosophy.

In concrete implementation of African metaphysics and in practical demonstration that African philosophy is a lived one, and implies man-man relationship of care and support, I developed a Pilgrimage Centre where much emphasis is given to religious activities and worship, caring and charity.

Here African metaphysics offers a challenge to the still lingering concept of man introduced into Western thought by the rationalists of the modern period, e.g. Feuerbach, Marx, Nietzsche and Sartre. These thinkers maintain that the human subject must seek birth through himself as absolute will to power, self-invention and freedom. In line with these, modern scientific thought has attempted to banish God and freedom from the world and has even attempted to practically exclude God from the world.

In contrast, African metaphysics has maintained the concept of beings dependent upon God. From our detailed interpretation and analysis leading to the African concept of beings and Being—*Chi-ne-ke, Ose-bu-luwa* and *Chi-ukwu*—, it is improbable that African thought will deviate from the direction it has already taken, namely, maintaining man's beholdenness to God. As I said earlier, African metaphysics as a religious metaphysics gives witness to man as *Homo religiosus*. The basis of this witness cannot but be a belief in and an acknowledgment of the Absolute Being. This belief leads us to an entire attitude of submission and respect to the Supreme Being, God (*Chi-ukwu*).

African metaphysics (*cf. Towards an Igbo Metaphysics*) therefore, in its distinctive feature, is as it were designed to uphold man's beholdenness to God rather than to proclaim man as rational absolute. The ground of this conclusion is obvious when we recall my indication in IGBO METAPHYSICS that thought is closely tied to the people's practical rather than theoretical way of life. Africans would more readily comprehend the idea of man's dependence on "our God" (*Chi-ukwu Anyi*), God who is actively present among us, the one whom we can conceive of and speak of in an anthropocentric manner, than they would comprehend the idea of a rational absolute which, in the last analysis, can be seen as the product of highly abstractive thinking.

The formalization of African metaphysics, which I have offered through the IGBO METAPHYSICS, must not and cannot be conceived in the same theoretical patterns that presuppose the rationalism akin to Aristotle's that led to his division of the sciences. It was such rationalism that Saint Augustine identified as the way of the philosophers in contrast to "Our" Christian way: a rationalism that subsequently called forth Aquinas' new synthesis.

By nature, African philosophy is a lived philosophy rather than a purely theoretical or scientific enterprise. Hence my formalization consisted in drawing out a rationalization of the lived experience of the people as expressed in their rituals, language and other cultural manifestations.

Philosophy of this kind leads one to the ideal of human experience based on the belief that all things are created by God and are ontologically good and deserve respect. This leads to a reflection on that God-man-world scheme which shows that African metaphysics testifies to the fact that the African is deeply religious, *Homo religiosus.*

THOUGHT AND ACTION (EPTAISM)

As I stated in my book *Peace to the Modern World,* after the presentation of the African metaphysical thought pattern, one must go further to show a concrete and practical actualization of this. In the same manner, arriving at the God-man-world scheme that characterizes African philosophy, leads one to the practical actualization in interplay between thought and action. This is what can be called EPTAISM, that is, Edeh's philosophy of Thought and Action.

This philosophy leads to African concept of theology which in turn leads to African religious tendencies. This is to say that the God-man scheme of reality must be concretized in the African way of life. In other words, the beholdenness of man to God must be experienced in African daily life.

Fr. Prof. E.M.P. Edeh C.S.Sp.

If God is *Chi-ne-ke*, the one who creates and is actually present in his creatures and He is also *Ose-bu-luwa*, the one whose active presence in the beings of experience means His care and support of these beings to the realization of their purpose, then, man in his beholdenness to God must be deeply involved in the care and support of man to the realization of man's purpose. God's care and support of man must be concretized in man's care and support for fellow man.

CHAPTER SIX

Practical and Effective Charity

The idea that «God's care and support for man must be concretized in man's care and support for fellow man» must be made to materialize at least, from my own point of view. As an African philosopher who has articulated African metaphysics that leads automatically to African theology and African religious tendencies, I have seriously endeavored to put thought into action.

Consequently, I arrived at the practical and effective charity as a concrete way of manifesting God's care and support for man.

If God as *Ose-bu-luwa* cares and supports man to the realization of his purpose, I must care and support my fellow man to the realization of his purpose and this leads to peace in his heart, peace in the society and to the modern world.

In other words, I must be a faithful instrument for the realization of God's care and support for man, and the best way to achieve this is no other than through a mission of practical and effective charity.

This mission, as I explained in my earlier book *Peace to the Modern World* (*cf.* page 6), is geared towards bringing care and supports wholeheartedly to man, especially the sick, the suffering, the abjectly poor and abandoned, the miserable but teaming youths in the African society and beyond who are in dire need of education.

It is in answer to God's call, and in pursuance of this mission that by the help of God I have established the Pilgrimage Centre, Elele, Nigeria since 1984. In this gigantic edifice I have the following units with special concentration on providing care and support to the sick, the suffering, the abjectly poor, the abandoned and miserable youths thus enabling them to have peace in their hearts:

A SUPER CENTRE FOR RELIGIOUS LIFE-ACTIVITIES AND WORSHIP

In this centre various kinds of religious activities, prayers and devotional events are going on 24 hours non-stop.

The centre, that began with a handful of the sick and suffering people recovering from the Nigerian civil war, has grown to hundreds of thousands and even millions of pilgrims. One who goes through the centre will certainly be convinceed that the Africans live their lives in total manifestation of man's beholdenness to God. People converging from various parts of the country and beyond come to pray, worship and adore God as *Chi-ukwu Anyi*. In many cases, pilgrims who have some personal problems and present them to God as *Ose-bu-luwa* have evidence to show that God heard their prayers and solved their problems. Such pilgrims come to give testimonies publicly for this.

A super centre for religious life-activities and worship like this is a concrete actualization of God's care and support for man, which leads definitively to the realization of man's purpose of creation. It certainly provides millions of human beings with peace in their heart as they actualize their purpose of creation.

It is a centre where peace reigns in the hearts of people, a centre where people with various kinds of problems conglomerate and have those problems removed. They settle with God and settle with fellow human beings, thus gaining true peace in their hearts, true peace in the society, and true peace in the modern world.

To perpetuate this healthy development namely, the maintenance of the centre as a source of peace raining in the hearts of many, various religious families have sprang up amidst the religious manifestations, devotional activities and worship. Thus I was divinely inspired to found:

- The Congregation of the Sisters of Jesus the Saviour, in 1985.
- The Fathers of Jesus the Saviour, in 1990.
- The Male Contemplatives of Jesus the Saviour, in 1991.
- The Female Contemplatives of Jesus the Saviour, in 2008.

The members of the above institutes of religious life are men and women who have devoted their entire lives to the service of God and humanity. Their charism is providing 24 hours of selfless adoration of God, i.e., man's beholdenness to God, and selfless service to human beings, thus bringing peace to the hearts of

Fr. Prof. E.M.P. Edeh C.S.Sp.

millions in the society whom peace have long eluded in the course of their unfortunate circumstances in life. It is through these religious men and women, members of these God-given foundations that my mission of practical and effective charity is conceived, planned and executed.

A CARING CENTRE PAR EXCELLENCE

Seeing the needs of the pilgrims who come to our Pilgrimage Centre with terrible problems ranging from the lack of the most basic needs of life to health and education problems, we developed the centre as a caring centre par excellence. This care is exercised in various ways and modalities, but suffice it to mention the following in this presentation:

- Umuogbenye Ward (care unit for the poorest of the people).
- Our Saviour Motherless Babies' Home.
- Free medical care for the abjectly poor and abandoned.
- Free Scholarships for the helpless and handicapped.
- Madonna International Charity Peace Award.

Umuogbenye Ward

The Umuogbenye Ward was established since 1984 at the very beginning of the Pilgrimage Centre. This is the unit that handles the poorest of the poor, the abjectly poor, the most abandoned in the society. These are people who cannot feed themselves and practically have nobody to feed them. Most of them have lost their families and relations. They have gone and are still going through protracted illnesses and are directed to come to Elele as the last resort for hope. Some are aged people who have no children to care for them and because there are little or no old peoples' homes in the society, the only alternative is to entrust themselves in the hands of our caring Centre. People of such categories come from various parts of the society.

The Umuogbenye unit is placed under the charge of a Rev. Sister who with her working team gathers such people daily, provides adequate food, clothing and shelter for them. She also aids each of them financially to enable him or her travel back to the family when due.

Another group of people who benefit from Umuogbenye Ward caring unit are those who, during the course of their travel run short of money. Such people are normally directed by passersby to visit the ward. On seeing the Sister in charge and explaining their problems, they get some charity money earmarked for such cases, just enough to take the stranded traveler to his or her destination.

The caring given to the innumerable people who are beneficiaries of Umuogbenye Ward do certainly provide support, happiness and above all peace to the hearts of thousands of souls who come to the ward, thus bringing peace to the modern world.

Our Saviour Motherless Babies' Home

Another unit for practical and effective charity is the motherless babies' home, established as early as 1989 in the Pilgrimage Centre. Children who were born and thrown away by very young girls hiding away from their parents, some born by mentally ill mothers, are rescued and cared for in the house. Also, some children are rescued from mothers who do not intend to nurse babies and are not prepared for it. Such children are nursed and properly cared for as part of our practical and effective charity programmes till they are adopted by childless couples who are ready and willing to provide proper parental care for them. The Sisters who work in the Motherless babies' home are devoted to providing care, love and support to these babies who otherwise would have been left to die for lack of parental care. Through this care and love, peace is poured in the hearts of the babies who are the future members of the society in the modern world.

Free Medical Care for the Abjectly Poor and Abandoned

Two groups of patients come every day to the Madonna University Teaching Hospital, located beside the Pilgrimage Centre, Elele. The first group consists of those who can by themselves pay for their medical treatments. The second group consists of those who are so poor that they can hardly eat not to talk of being able to pay even a penny for their medical treatments.

We have many cases of this second group every day. Nevertheless they are properly treated free of charge under our practical and effective charity programme. Very costly life saving surgeries have been administered free of charge. The care of free medication and free surgeries are fully given to those who cannot help themselves in the society. This is a veritable source of giving peace to the world through the mission of practical and effective charity.

Free Scholarships for the Helpless and Handicapped

Another area where we exhibit our practical and effective charity scheme is our policy of enabling abjectly poor students to study in our tertiary institutions free of charge. Many of them study in our Universities—Madonna University and Caritas University. Our standing scholarship programme for all handicapped students—the blind, crippled, deaf, and dumb— has yielded a tremendous amount of positive and encouraging results. Since the inception of our Polytechnic in 1989, we have graduated many blind and crippled students, thus giving them a good start in life and a new lease of life. Suffice to say that the students who are beneficiaries to our scholarship programme have gained immensely from our practical and effective love, care and support. This should lead them to have peace in their hearts and thus contribute to peace in the modern world.

Madonna International Charity Peace Award

A very vital step in the direction of practical and effective charity which God has effected through my humble instrumentality is the institution of the Madonna International Charity Peace Award programme. In November 2006, we organized the First International Convention of Experts and Intellectuals, hosted at the Pilgrimage Centre, Elele. The Convention, which lasted for seven days, was attended by distinguished personalities drawn from various countries: United States of America, Colombia, England, Germany, Poland, Australia, India, South Africa and Nigeria.

One of the highlights of the convention was the official inauguration of what I called Madonna International Charity Peace Award programme. The origin of this can be traced back to my dear Mother *Mama Omeogo,* who a few days before she died in 1996, handed over to me all her savings, a total of ₦ 360,000 (three hundred and sixty thousand naira), with the instruction that it should be used not only in giving charity to the helpless and the abandoned, but must also be used to instigate and encourage practicing charity in its grass roots. This is now being spear-headed by me and supported through our major institutions, namely: The Catholic Prayer Ministry worldwide, The Pilgrimage Centre in Elele, Nigeria, Madonna University and Caritas University, all in Nigeria, as well as OSISATECH[1] Polytechnic and OSISATECH College of Education.

This award, no matter how small, is to be given to whoever in the whole world has distinguished himself or herself in achieving peace in the modern world (peace in the hearts of many in the society) through his or her works of practical and effective charity, that is, instigating and encouraging practicing charity in its grass roots through unreserved and selfless care and support of the most helpless members of the society

---

[1] Our Saviour Institute of Science, Agriculture and Technology. *(Ed.)*

leading to peace in the hearts of many and thus peace to the modern world.

This is an award that has begun in a small way but hopefully, will grow to be world renowned like the Nobel Peace Prize Award of Oslo in Norway. Note that it cannot be politicized, since, it is essentially a charity peace award based on works of practical and effective charity; not only practicing effective charity in the grass roots but inducing others to practice it.

After ten years of prayerful reflections and consultations with my superiors, I decided to inaugurate the charity award as one of the key events in our mission of practical and effective charity. The Award was blessed and officially instituted in Elele with a pontifical Holy Mass officiated by the Bishop of Port Harcourt Diocese in Nigeria, Most Rev. Dr. A. O. Makozi.

International persons from various countries were selected as board members of the Award. They include people from England, Germany, United States of America, Holland, Austria, and Africa, especially Nigeria.

Fr. Prof. E.M.P. Edeh C.S.Sp.

CONCLUSIONS

As I come to the end of this presentation, let me go a little back to my point of departure. African metaphysics, as shown through our articulation of IGBO METAPHYSICS, demonstrates that with the notion of being drawn from the concept of man, African metaphysics is a theological metaphysics. The man-centered concept of being is at the same time a religious view of reality with God as the ultimate source and man as a dependent entity. Hence, African metaphysics must bring us to African theology and African religious way of life. In this little work, I have also tried to show that the African concept of being has led us into the African concept of reality which witnesses man as *Homo religiosus*. The basis of this witness is a belief in or an acknowledgment of the Absolute Being, *Chi-ukwu* who is *Chi-ne-ke*, and at the same time, *Ose-bu-luwa*.

As *Ose-bu-luwa*, the relationship between God and man is a religious one. Man in the lived experience is closely united to the Absolute that he cannot but always manifest his beholdenness to God. And this is why a typical African is deeply religious. His religious life and tendencies lead him to the realization of man's purpose of being by bringing peace to his heart. Consequently, peace in the hearts of many in the society leads to the realization of peace in the modern society, and peace in the modern world.

From this presentation it is evident that: From deep religious life and activities spring up the devoted religious men and women who through their lives perpetuate the work and the mission of practical and effective charity.

As we have seen, they do this through their devotional and unreservedly caring for the *Umuogbenye* (the poorest of the poor). This is evident from their special care for the helpless motherless babies, their providing free medical care for the abjectly poor and scholarship to the abandoned in the society. The handicapped, namely, the crippled, the blind, deaf and dumb are picked up and given free care and education to the tertiary level. Above all the sense of endeavoring to practice this type of boundless charity is instigated in the society through the institution of the Madonna International Charity Peace Award.

All these, to my own understanding, are the most effective ways of entrenching peace in the hearts of many, peace in societies and therefore peace in the modern world.

Effecting peace in the modern world today does not necessarily mean stopping ongoing wars between nations. In this modern world hardly can one find nations quickly engaging into wars, only in rare cases can one or two nations be so stupid as to engage themselves in wars. Nobody in the civilized nations wants to go to war where any can die. It is only in very few cases that one or two nations are deceived into war by external influences from big nations who can never come out to fight and run the risk of getting their people killed or be handicapped for life. As I said, it is very rare in this modern world of high scientific and technological advancement when no one wants any-thing other than to enjoy rather than suffer. But even where people in the society have the tendencies to go to war against other, the practice and spirit of practical and effective charity can stop that tendency. For the kind of care given through practical and effective charity ushers in happiness, rest of mind and peace to the individuals and families in the society. It provides care and support to many and the peace and support spread from individuals to many and from many to many more in the society.

Monday Anih cured of mouth tumor free of charge.

The sight of a young man whose protruding tumor was removed free of charge through our caring and support in Madonna University Teaching Hospital Nigeria, radiates the peace in the society that many politicians with all their money and idiosyncrasies cannot give.

Beholding a blind boy, one of our blind students, Barrister Osuji Vincent, who graduated from OSISATECH Polytechnic on our scholarship scheme, later finished up as a lawyer and is now working in Federal Ministry of Justice, Abuja. His presence in the Court and intervention in a case for a client certainly rains peace in the hearts of thousands in the society and thus peace in the modern world.

Barrister Osuji Vincent.

From the foregoing it is abundantly clear that drawing from African metaphysics, as a lived philosophy, brings us to African theology expressed in the religious life and activities of man shown in the mystery of God's dealing with man and man's beholdenness to God as *Chi-ne-ke* as well as *Ose-bu-luwa*. And it, necessarily leads to the mission of practical and effective charity, which is a concrete actualization of God's care and support for His creatures to the realization of the purpose of their creation. This is true peace in the hearts of man, which constitutes true peace in the modern world.

A super center for religious life-activities surely leads to peace in the modern world: a centre where peace reigns in the hearts of people as they conglomerate with all kinds of problems and settle with God and with fellow human beings, thus gaining true peace in their hearts, true peace in the society and true peace in the modern world.

A caring center par excellence that provides care and support to the poorest of the poor in the society—the motherless babies home, free medical care to the poor and the abandoned, scholarship to the helpless and handicapped, and charity award to encourage privileged individuals from all over the world to embark on practical and effective charity: All these certainly must bring peace to the hearts of innumerable human beings, peace to the society and hence peace to the modern world.

If one, through practical and effective charity, cares and supports the lowly group of human beings in the society as are cared for in the above mentioned charity programmes, there's no way in which you as a head of state will agree to declare war when you know that every war in this modern world must involve killing and destruction of not the rich and the important people in the society but the poor, the lower group in the society. In the event of wars the ones who are pushed to the warfronts are usually the masses. It is the masses who in most cases become victims of uprising, victims of sporadic bombing in the society during the outbreak of any war.

Hence it is clear that practical and effective charity brings peace to not only the sick, the suffering, the abandoned in the society. It also brings peace to the lower group of people in the society of the modern world who would have suffered greatly during any kind of war or uprising.

Even in a labour or civil demonstration, in most cases, it is the lowest group of people who come out and parade with banners under sunshine and rain while the leaders remain in their offices and homes directing people and manipulating affairs. Meanwhile the poor, the lowly, the sick in the society suffer and even die as victims of the demonstration whose origin they may not know.

Hence practical and effective charity if maintained even on the level of the very poor, sick and suffering, leads to peace in our society.

So if you are in politics or in any leadership position, practical and effective charity demands that in serious consideration of the sick, the dying, the suffering, the lowly, the abjectly poor and the abandoned, you will not only allow peace to reign but you must foster peace in the hearts of the society. Thus practical and effective charity leads to peace in the modern world.

The Question of World Peace

If the African philosophy of being (*Ife-di*) as typified in IGBO METAPHYSICS is maintained and practiced properly, the perennial problem of world peace becomes a thing of the past.

The amount of wealth and energy spent on amassing both nuclear and non-nuclear weapons in readiness for the *fateful day of massive destruction of man by man*, if used to promote and generate the means of *practical and effective charity, let peace and tranquility reign in the hearts of millions in the present day society*, through justice and reconciliation, the problem of world peace will certainly be an overcome problem. Is it not true?

Fr. Prof. E.M.P. Edeh C.S.Sp.

The question of developing and keeping of nuclear weapons whether as a means of defence or a means of attacking and destroying man who is "good that is" and who deserves to be *treated with the ideal of human dignity*, will be handled with the utmost moral concern. If the world accepts the notion of man as "good that is" then man is bound not to destroy fellow man, rather man in his beholdeness to God must treat fellow man as good that is because of man's having been created by God the source of all goodness.

INDEX OF NAMES

AQUINAS, ST. THOMAS – Italian Dominican friar and priest, and an immensely influential philosopher and theologian in the tradition of scholasticism (1225-1274).

ARISTOTLE – Greek philosopher (384 B.C.-322 B.C.).

BERGSON, HENRI-LOUIS – A major French philosopher, influential especially in the first half of the 20th century (1859-1941).

HEGEL, GEORGE WILHELM FRIEDRICH – German philosopher and a major figure in German Idealism (1770-1831).

HEIDEGGER, MARTIN – German philosopher, known for his existential and phenomenological explorations of the "question of Being" (1889-1976).

HERACLITUS – Greek philosopher (535 B.C.-475 B.C.).

LONERGAN, BERNARD – Canadian Jesuit priest, philosopher, and theologian regarded by some as one of the most important thinkers of the twentieth century (1904-1984).

MONISTS – Monism is a (western) philosophical position which argues that the variety of existing things can be explained in terms of a single reality or substance.

NIETZSCHE, FRIEDRICH – German philologist, philosopher, cultural critic, poet and composer (1844-1900).

Fr. Prof. E.M.P. Edeh C.S.Sp.

PARRINDER, EDWARD GEOFFREY – African scholar, who wrote *African Traditional Religion,* which second edition was published in London in 1962.

PARMENIDES – Greek philosopher, founder of the Eleatic school of philosophy, active in the earlier part of the 5th century B.C.

PLATO – Greek philosopher (427 B.C. – 347 B.C.).

SPINOZA, BARUCH – Jewish-Dutch philosopher (1632-1677).

STOICS – A member of an original Greek school of philosophy, founded by Zeno about 308 B.C., believing that God determined everything for the best and that virtue is sufficient for happiness.

WHITEHEAD, ALFRED NORTH – An English mathematician and philosopher (1861-1947).

REFERENCES

Rev. Fr. Prof. E.M.P Edeh. 1985. *Towards an Igbo Metaphysics*. Chicago: Loyola University Press.

_____, ed. 2004. *Madonna University, an Institution with a Difference*. Enugu: Our Saviour Press Ltd.

_____, ed. n.d. *The Catholic Prayer Ministry and the Pilgrimage Centre of Eucharistic Adoration and Special Marian Devotion*. Enugu: Our Saviour Press Ltd.

Mother John Bosco Kalu, SJS. 2004. *Peace to the Modern Society*. Enugu: Our Saviour Press Ltd.

Very Rev. Fr. Prof. Emmanuel M.P Edeh, C.S.Sp. 2007. *Peace to the Modern World*. London: Minutemann Press.

Fr. Prof. E.M.P. Edeh C.S.Sp.

BIBLIOGRAPHY

Achebe, Chinua. *No Longer at Ease.* Greenwich, Conn.: Fawcett Publication, 1969.

_____. *Things Fall Apart.* Greenwich, Conn.: Fawcett Publication, 1959.

Aristotle. *Basic works.* Edited by Richard McKeon. New York: Random House, 1941.

Egbujie, Innocent I. "The Hermeneutics of the African Traditional Culture." Ph.D. Dissertation, Boston College, 1976.

Ezeanya, S. N. "God, Spirit and the Spiritual World." In *Biblical Revelation and African Beliefs.* London: Lutherworth Press, 1969.

Glison, Etienne and Thomas D. Langan. *Modern Philosophy: Descartes to Kant.* New York: Random House, 1963.

Idowu E. Bolgi. *Olodumare: God in Yoruba Belief.* Lagos: Federal Ministry of Information, 1963.

July, Robert W. *A History of the African People.* 3rd ed. New York: Charles Scribner & Sons, 1984.

Mbiti John S. *African Religions and Philosophy.* New York: Double Day, 1970.

Niven Cyril Rex. *A Short History of Nigeria.* London: Longmans; Green, and Co., 1952.

Obiego, Cosmas. "Igbo Idea of Life and Death in Relation to Christian God." Ph.D. Dissertation, Pontifica Urban University de Propaganda Fide, Rome, 1971.

Okpaloka, P. "The Supreme Being in Igbo Religion." Exercitatio Practica, Bigard Memorial Seminary, Enugu, 1979.

Pegis, Anton C. *Introduction to St. Thomas Aquinas.* New York: Random House, 1965.

Shaw, C. Thurstan. *Igbo-Ukwu: An Account of Archeological Discoveries in Eastern Nigeria.* 2 vols. Evaston: Northwestern University Press, 1970.

Talbot, Percy A. *Peoples of Southern Nigeria.* 2 vols. London: Frank Cass, 1969.

Thomas, Northcote W. Law and Culture of the Asaba District, 4th vol. of *Anthropological Report on Ibo-speaking Peoples of Nigeria.* 6 vols. London: Harrison, 1914.

Uchendu, Victor C. *The Igbo of South East Nigeria* (Case studies in Cultural Anthropology). New York: Holth Rinehart and Winston, 1965.